GW01180108

Original title:

The Winter Waddle: How to Walk on Ice

Author: Liam Sterling

ISBN HARDBACK: 978-9916-94-194-2
ISBN PAPERBACK: 978-9916-94-195-9

Harmony in Frigid Steps

Step one, a graceful glide,
But oh dear, I must decide!
Tip-toeing like a feather light,
Or pressing down with all my might?

Each move, a curious ballet,
Arms flail, oh what a display!
Watch out, world, I'm on a spree,
I'll stick the landing, wait and see!

Dancing on Diamond Dust

Oh look, it shines beneath my feet,
A frosty dance, no way to cheat!
I twist and twirl, a balletic mess,
With every step, I must confess.

My friends all laugh, and so do I,
As I attempt to glide and fly.
The ice won't budge, it loves to tease,
I'm stuck in place, oh, what a freeze!

Chilling Charm

To slip and slide is quite the art,
With charm and grace, I’ll take my part.
A friendly penguin lends a paw,
As I'm about to take a fall.

I huff and puff, reclaim my stance,
Inviting luck, I dare to dance.
A shuffle here, a wiggle there,
Ah, the thrill of icy air!

Slippery Symphony

A symphony of squeaks I make,
With every shaky move I take.
The ground beneath, a playful foe,
With every waltz, I steal the show.

A cha-cha here, a quick duck dive,
I laugh and lurch, how will I thrive?
In this frosty concert so divine,
Each slip and slide, a twist of mine!

Frostbitten Finesse

I stepped outside, oh what a thrill,
A ballet dancer, with little skill.
My feet, they slide, like a fish on ice,
Should I grab a stick? This is not so nice.

With arms all flailing, I try to stand,
But gravity's pulling like a heavy hand.
The neighbors laugh, oh what a sight,
As I moonwalk backwards into the night.

Eloquent Ice Trails

I strut like a penguin, proud and fine,
Each step a dance, though not divine.
I tip and I toe, my moves are quite grand,
A slip here and there, it wasn't my plan.

With every lurch, my ego deflates,
Falling on patches of ice that awaits.
I’m an ice explorer, so brave and bold,
Though my dignity's frozen, it’s still mine to hold!

Ballet of the Brave

The stage is set with glistening sheen,
I launch with flair, like a frosty machine.
Twirl and spin, then whoops, a slip!
Round and round, on a slippery trip.

My toes are pointed, my focus so keen,
Then down I go, a frosty routine.
A neighbor cheers, “Encore!” as I fall,
The ice is my stage, I’m having a ball!

Glacial Grip

Caution's advised, they tell me so,
But I’m a thrill-seeker, and off I go.
I grip the rail, so solid and true,
Like a fish on ice, it’s a slippery view.

My friends are giggling, I give them a show,
With each little shuffle, I steal the glow.
“Look, I can glide!” I boast with pride,
Then down I tumble, it’s a comical ride!

Fractured Beauty Beneath Snow

Upon the ice, my feet do glide,
Like a penguin on a wild ride.
A slip, a slide, oh what a dance,
With every move, I take a chance.

The world is white, a snowy quilt,
One moment proud, the next, I wilt.
Together we tumble, the ground takes a shot,
Laughing and gasping, is this skill, or not?

A graceful spin turns into a fall,
I’m soaring high, then feeling small.
Laughter echoes with each cold smack,
Each time I slip, I just bounce back.

So here I slip, and here I sway,
Feeling like a star in disarray.
Fractured beauty in icy land,
Just hoping to make it, without a hand.

Sleek Silhouettes on Ice

Like shadows gliding, sleek and sly,
We aim for grace, but oh, we fly!
A wobble here, a lurch there,
Each step's a riddle, a slippery affair.

Skates might be better, but I can't fit,
So I shuffle along, just trying to sit.
Wide-leg stances, foot paths askew,
Creating a painting, an abstract view.

Oh, look at us, a moving show,
A comic play, putting on a glow.
falling often, like leaves that sway,
Yet laughter rises like sun on gray.

With every tumble, a tale unfolds,
Cold cheeks and giggles, a joy that holds.
Sleek silhouettes, we are a sight,
Turning the ice from fright to delight.

Walking in the Cold Glow

With boots so big, I plod along,
Hoping my feet don’t prove me wrong.
The ice is sparkling, a sly, soft tease,
But one little slip brings me to my knees.

I jiggle and sway, a dance with fate,
Each step's a gamble, oh, isn’t it great?
Wobbly strut, I channel my inner duck,
Like a quack-quack queen, I run out of luck.

Frosty breath makes a cloud in the air,
Giggles arise as I stumble with flair.
I’m not quite graceful, but what can I say?
It’s a winter ballet in a comical way.

From cozy mittens to layers so thick,
I’m bundled up tightly, just waiting to trick.
So here’s to the laughter the ice brings us all,
With each little slip, I just want to crawl.

Serenity in Slippery Solitude

One foot out, I take my chance,
A wobble here, a curious dance.
The ground beneath, a glassy foe,
With every step, I steal the show.

A laugh erupts from those nearby,
As legs splay wide, I dare to fly.
With arms like wings, I take my flight,
A silly sight in crisp moonlight.

Icebound Elegance

In fancy boots, I try to glide,
But oh! My balance I cannot abide.
A penguin's strut, I mimic with glee,
Slipping and sliding, all eyes on me.

With graceful waves, I question fate,
Each tiny step, a fearsome debate.
It's art, I claim, a sight divine,
A performance no one can confine.

Swaying with the Chilled Air

The chilly breeze teases my face,
As I shuffle and sway in a frozen race.
A frosty embrace, I tread with flair,
Wobbling gently, if only to care.

Friends chuckle loud at my frosty plight,
They twirl with grace, but I'm not in sight.
A spin and a slip, I claim my throne,
Majestic in chaos, yet all on my own.

Frozen Paths and Delicate Moves

On this shiny path, I'm brave yet meek,
With cautious steps and a wobble chic.
Each crack and crunch makes my heart race,
Oh slippery floor, what a wild chase!

A ballet of blunders, with arms akimbo,
I aim for elegance but land like a limbo.
With laughter around, I charm the crowd,
As I pirouette, chaotic and proud.

The Grace of Winter Steps

With each step I take, I slide,
I waddle, I wobble, it's quite the ride.
My arms flail like flags, in funny retreat,
As I dance with delight on this tricky street.

I spot a small patch of glittering sheen,
My feet make a move, oh what a scene!
I try to look cool, but I end up a mess,
With a pirouette that results in distress.

Snowflakes descend, a comedic banner,
My balance unsteady, like a drunken planner.
Each step is a gamble, a chance to fall down,
A circus of laughter, not a frown in town.

So in this frosty realm of slippery fun,
I’ll glide with the giggles and cheer under the sun.
Though elegance flies right out the door,
I’ll waddle through winter and always ask for more.

Glacial Whispers

Listen closely, the ice will tell,
Of tumbles and trips, a frosty carousel.
Each whispering crack is a giggle profound,
As I sway to the music of slippery ground.

A penguin's finesse is what I pursue,
But all I can muster is a bumbling queue.
My legs, they are noodles, all jiggly and cold,
A ballet of chaos, as my tale unfolds.

Embracing the freeze, I channel my stride,
While clueless bystanders snicker and chide.
I slip and I slide, I'm the star of this show,
With laughter as winter's delightful tableau.

Oh, glacial allure, you crafty old hen,
You pull off the stunts as you giggle again.
In this frosty ballet, we all share a grin,
Dancing and slipping, let the fun begin!

Ballet on the Glassy Nature

A ballet begins on ice so refined,
Yet my graceful motions are barely aligned.
With every slick glide, I pirouette clumsy,
Giggling alongside my friends who are fumbly.

Arms flailing like sails caught in a gale,
My elegance ebbs with each slippery trail.
I'll leap and I'll tumble with laughter so loud,
Each fumble a highlight, I'm proud to be proud.

Chassé to the left, then a swish to the right,
I twirl like a tornado, what a hilarious sight!
The audience chuckles with glee at my plight,
As I glide on this canvas of sparkles so bright.

So let's take a bow for this quirky show,
With thrills on ice, where the laughter can flow.
Our winter ballet, a dance of delight,
With some stumbles embraced, it's a pure joyous flight!

Sliding Symphony

Hear the notes of my slipping anthem, played,
A symphony where elegance is delayed.
With each little waddle, I take to the stage,
Creating a masterpiece of wintery rage.

My knees buckle low, I'm a sight to behold,
Learning the rhythms, both timid and bold.
But with every misstep, I find I can laugh,
Turning my mishaps to joy on this path.

The trumpets of laughter, the strings of the frost,
Each time I fall down, I'm not really lost.
With claps from the snowflakes and cheers in the air,
My sliding adventures are full of good flair.

So let's lift our mugs to this frosty ballet,
For slipping and sliding, the playful display.
With winter composing this joyous refrain,
We all dance together in laughter and rain!

Starlit Slips

Under the moon, we take our chance,
Each step we take is a clumsy dance.
Arms flailing wide, a balance test,
We giggle hard, it's our icy quest.

Skates on our shoes, what could go wrong?
A hop, a skip, we're not very strong.
Landing in snow, we burst into laughter,
Making new memories, we chase after.

With hats askew and mittens lost,
We'll brave the path, no matter the cost.
Like penguins sliding, we zoom and glide,
Who needs finesse when you have pride?

So come join us, don't be shy,
On this slick path, we'll soar and fly.
In jumbled fun, our spirits ignite,
As we dance on ice, under starlit light.

Glimmer of Grace on Ice

Dressed in layers, we step outside,
Hoping for grace with every glide.
Ahead of us lies a shiny sheet,
But stability just might retreat.

With a little hop and a wild twist,
Down we go, it's hard to resist.
Laughter erupts from the frosty ground,
As we flail about, no grace can be found.

Our friends stand by, in fits of glee,
Watching our dance, not quite carefree.
We wave and wobble, our joy unmasked,
In this chilly play, we've found our task.

In giggles and tumbles, our hearts unite,
Finding fun on this slippery site.
With every misstep, we shout and cheer,
For in these moments, winter feels clear.

Dance of the Frosty Spirits

Chilling winds whisper, come take the leap,
With frosty spirits, we'll find the heap.
Our feet start to slide, our laughter soars,
As we trip and tumble, we'll dance on all fours.

Like wobbly ducks, we shuffle along,
With each little slip, we hum a new song.
Fingers crossed tight, we hope for a land,
Where ice turns to laughter, hand in hand.

Carefree and wild, we glide on the run,
Chasing the snowflakes, oh what fun!
Epic wipeouts that make us all bright,
As we twirl like dancers in the moonlight.

So let's embrace this frosty ballet,
With slips and slides, we'll be a cabaret.
Together we'll laugh till the day is done,
In this dance of spirits, we shine like the sun.

Navigating Winter's Slick

With socks on our feet and boots that squeak,
The ice gives a grin, oh what a peek.
We take a step, then a slip and a slide,
Our hearts well-equipped for this thrilling ride.

Each shuffle and stumble is wrapped in cheer,
For winter’s slick dance brings us all near.
We wink at the ground, as it’s calling our name,
In a raucous performance, we’re all part of the game.

Hopes that we won’t fall flat on our face,
Yet giggles erupt, we’re the clumsy grace.
Navigating slicks, we jazz up our game,
With every misstep, we shout out the same.

So arm in arm, we’ll waddle on through,
To find the bright side as we slip too.
In this winter chaos, there’s joy we demand,
With laughter and ice, we make our stand.

Frosty Waltz of Resilience

On a frozen lake, I take my stand,
With boots like penguins, oh so grand.
A slip, a slide, a graceful fall,
A dance with ice, I heed its call.

With arms flailing, I try to sway,
Like a drunken ballerina at play.
My friends all laugh, they cannot help,
As I juggle laugh and melted kelp.

I tiptoe here, I jiggle there,
With every step, a freezing dare.
A winter's breeze, a frosty kick,
In this ballet, I learn the trick.

But through the slips, I find my groove,
In this brisk chaos, I start to move.
A frosty waltz, my heart's delight,
On icy paths, my spirit's flight.

Steps in Shimmering Silence

A glistening path, I start to roam,
Where ice and snow call me to home.
My feet are cautious, my heart in flight,
With every shiver, I grip so tight.

I step on glimmers, oh so slick,
Trying hard not to fall, it's tricky, quick.
Like careful crabs, we sidestep glide,
With laughter shared, we brave the slide.

A tumble here, a giggle there,
Slipping and sliding without a care.
The ground is still, the air is cold,
But with each wobble, our courage unfolds.

In this frozen land, we find our cheer,
Forget the chill, we've nothing to fear.
Through all the mishaps, we share a grin,
For life's a dance, let the fun begin!

Icy Overture

Upon this stage of shimmering white,
I take a step, oh what a fright!
The ground beneath, a treacherous tease,
With every slide, my hopes to freeze.

My feet are dancers, they twirl and spin,
But gravity pulls, oh where to begin?
With a puff of breath and a hopeful grin,
I choose to laugh, it's all in good fun!

A flurry of snow, my fluffy friend,
As I conquer slopes that seem to bend.
With bumps and jumps, I sing my song,
In icy overtures, where we belong.

The show goes on with every freeze,
In laughter, joy, and winter's breeze.
So take my hand, let’s glide and sway,
On this slippery stage, come what may!

Balance Amidst the Chill

In frosty air, I find my path,
With careful steps, I avoid the wrath.
The ice ahead, it gleams and grins,
As wobbly warriors retreat, but not give in.

My boots a-shuffle, my heart a-thump,
I move like a goat, with a cautious jump.
While friends beside me giggle and cheer,
I channel my courage, push away fear.

A slip, a slide, down I go,
But laughter erupts, as spirits flow.
We leap and dance on this icy thrill,
Balancing joy amidst the chill.

From here to there, we skate with glee,
In this winter game, we all agree.
With every stumble, we smile and cheer,
For life is a dance, and ice makes it clear!

The Art of Balancing on Snow's Edge

With careful steps, I tread most slow,
A dance of balance, a frosty show.
One foot glides forth, the other slips back,
I’m dodging a fall with each little crack.

My arms like wings, I flail a lot,
A penguin suit would help, I thought!
With every move, the laughter grows,
A figure skating mishap in winter’s prose.

Each twist and turn, my heart does race,
With frozen ground and a frantic pace,
Should I try a jump? Oh what a goof!
I land on my rear, my own private roof!

Yet here I stand, with pride, I beam,
It's a comedy sketch, or so it seems.
For every slip and every trip,
Life's icy path keeps me on this trip.

Whispering Footsteps in Frost

The ground is glazed, a mirror wide,
I take a breath, my heart a guide.
With tiny shuffles, like a baby deer,
Might need some help, or maybe a steer.

I whisper softly, 'Please hold me tight,'
As ice gives way to my brief fright.
With every step, I tip and sway,
My feet have truly lost their way!

A squirrel laughs from its lofty tree,
As I weave like a drunk, carefree.
Should I grab a pole? Or just stay cool?
I think I'm making a winter fool!

But every slide brings joy to me,
As I embrace my slippery spree.
A giggle escapes, oh what a thrill,
In this frozen fun, I fit the bill.

Choreography of Cold

A ballet upon the icy floor,
With every movement, I crave for more.
I stretch and glide, my toes get bold,
Twisting and turning, in a dance of cold.

But soon I'm lost, the ice a tease,
My pirouette turns to a wheezy wheeze.
Flailing limbs, I strike a pose,
The wind now laughs, and off it blows!

I check my style, all turned around,
Am I 'dancing' or just falling down?
Each slip and plop feels like a score,
A choreography of cold I adore!

Yet in this folly, I find such glee,
Icebound ballet is pure comedy.
For laughter reigns in every slip,
In this frozen waltz, we all take a trip.

Elegance on a Silver Sheet

How graceful I feel on this shiny gloss,
Each step a whisper, but wait, I toss!
My feet take flight, all hope seems lost,
I dance with danger at a slippery cost.

Like fashion models, we strut with flair,
One slip away from a dramatic air.
With legs akimbo and laughter loud,
We're a merry troupe, making snow proud.

I spin like a top, with arms wide spread,
A graceful arc, or a tumble instead?
Yet in the flurry of frosty mischance,
Each fall feels like my own winter dance.

So here we twirl on this shimmering ground,
Each splat and slide is a joyous sound.
With winter's charm and a wink of fate,
Our elegance blooms, never to abate.

Crafting Confidence on the Thin Sheet

With each step, I glide and sway,
Convinced I'm a star in a ballet.
But oh! What's this? A slip and slide,
I'm down on my bottom, there's nowhere to hide!

I waddle like a duck, so proud and bright,
While neighbors snicker, oh what a sight!
Yet laughing at me, they can't resist,
For falling is part of the fun on this list!

With gloves on my hands and a beanie tight,
I plan my next move, not losing my fight.
Step by step, I try to play cool,
In this frosty dance, I won't be a fool!

So here's to the ice, both slippery and grand,
Where tumbles and laughter go hand in hand.
I'll skate through my fears, on this sheet so fine,
Crafting confidence, one fall at a time!

Frosty Adventures Await

With boots laced up, I'm feeling spry,
It's time for adventure beneath the gray sky.
The ice calls my name, oh what a tease,
I'll tiptoe like a cat, with grace and a breeze!

A hot cocoa dream, I clutch it tight,
But as I step forward, there's a laugh in sight.
One foot goes left, the other swings wide,
I'm careening down, where's my icy ride?

With a bounce and a plop, I land in a heap,
The laughter of friends, oh so sweet!
A frosty adventure, I'll never forget,
For falling on ice is a fun little threat.

With hands on my knees, I rise from the ice,
My friends cheering loudly, oh isn't it nice?
I'll conquer this patch, with bells on my toes,
For frosty adventures, each winter one knows!

Poetry of the Icy Walk

In quiet layers, the ice does gleam,
A canvas for chaos, a slip-and-slide theme.
I step out with swagger, I'm feeling bold,
But gravity laughs, as I tumble uncontrolled!

Like a turkey on skates, I flail and I flop,
My friends cry in laughter, they just cannot stop.
With arms flapping wildly, I dance on my toes,
In the poetry of ice, the drama just flows!

Oh, the rhythms we find in the chill of the air,
Where a wobble's a waltz, and we don't have a care.
Each slip tells a story, each fall a new rhyme,
In this hilarious saga, we're joking through time!

So here's to the winters, where laughter unfolds,
And poetry blooms on these frosty cold roads.
With each icy hiccup, we find joy in the freeze,
The art of the slip is a humorous breeze!

Soft Steps on the Glinting Surface

Creeping on ice with a hopeful grin,
Each soft step I take feels like a win.
With slippery dreams of a graceful sway,
I'm a comedy act on this glimmering play!

Penguin-like struts, I chant in delight,
But my boots have conspired to start a big fight.
One moment I'm up, the next I'm on ground,
This soft-glinting surface has joyfully wound.

Laughter erupts as I shimmy and slide,
While friends gather round, they're loving the ride.
Each tiptoe's a tale, each tumble a cheer,
Together we'll dance through this wintery sphere!

As stars twinkle down and the moon shines low,
We wobble and wiggle through cold winds that blow.
With soft steps we learn to embrace every fall,
In this game of ice, we're having a ball!

Ballet of the Brave on Ice

With graceful twirls and shaky knees,
They glide and dip, oh what a tease!
A little slip, a face like cheese,
The crowd erupts with happy wheeze!

One leg in front, the other behind,
Their confidence grows, but oh, they grind!
They leap and spin, they feel so blind,
As gravity shows, it’s not so kind!

A pirouette turns into a flop,
They slide and laugh, they can’t just stop!
With arms flailing in a cyclist’s prop,
They tumble around, then slowly drop!

Yet through the falls, they still perform,
With every glide, new moves are born!
In this brave ballet, they learn to swarm,
A dance of laughter against the norm!

Frosty Feats of Foot

Two boots collide, what a strange sight,
As they shuffle and slip with all their might!
Hopping around, a comical fight,
Who knew that ice could cause such fright?

Each step forward feels like a dare,
As they wiggle and wobble without a care!
With a sudden swerve, they twist in midair,
And land with a thud, a laugh to share!

They create an art, a blundering show,
With each little slip, their movements flow!
A frosty ballet, oh how they glow,
In the theater of ice, they steal the show!

Giggles and shrieks fill the chilly space,
As they struggle to find their rhythm and grace!
With every mishap, they laugh in embrace,
In frosty feats, they've found their place!

A Dance of Caution

With eyes on the floor, not a glance above,
They shuffle and slide, as if in love!
Each step is measured, a balance glove,
In careful rhythms, they fit like a dove!

Not a skater’s glide, but a careful tread,
As thoughts of safety swirl in their head!
Who needs to leap? Just a gentle spread,
With cautious glances, no ice is wed!

The art of pausing, a slow-motion cue,
Like turtles in dance, they move with a dew!
A step too far, what could they do?
With giggles erupting, they start anew!

In this honed ballet, they find their flow,
With laughter and slips, they put on a show!
A dance of caution, oh how they glow,
An ice-capped romp, ‘neath the winter’s snow!

Glacial Waltz of the Wanderer

With a glacial pulse, they sway and twist,
On a frosty floor, they cannot resist!
A dazzling glide, yet a comical list,
As down they go, a tumbler's tryst!

They twirl about like leaves in flight,
Wobbling and giggling, what a sight!
With every misstep, they crawl with delight,
In this icy brawl, they're holding tight!

A shuffle here, a sidestep there,
With their flailing arms, they giggle and stare!
A glimmer of grace hidden somewhere,
As they dance over ice, in cold, crisp air!

So let's raise a toast to the wobbly crew,
In glacial waltz, they push on through!
With laughter and tumbles, they bid adieu,
To a world of ice, where dreams come true!

Crisp Treads

Crunchy white beneath my shoe,
A dance with danger, a slip, a woo!
Laughing as I glide with ease,
Like a penguin on a frosty breeze.

Snowflakes swirl and giggles rise,
Trying hard to play it wise.
Arm flailing, a frosty ballet,
Just don't let your pride decay!

My friends observe, they point and cheer,
As I stumble, oh dear, oh dear!
With every step, I break the mold,
Ice is slippery, or so I'm told.

But onward I go, with valor true,
A crinkle of laughter, a slip or two.
One more step, a final leap,
Into the snowdrift, and laughter deep!

Cascading Over Cold

Wobbling like a newborn deer,
The world ahead begins to leer.
A graceful glide? Not quite today,
More like a circus on display!

Each step a mini-adventure bold,
Shuffle, slide, a sight to behold.
With flailing limbs and giggles shared,
Who knew that ice could leave us scared?

I twirl and spin, oh what a show,
A perfect fall, my skills now grow.
With a thud and a chuckle, I land,
Snowflakes laugh at my clumsy stand.

The cold may bite, but laughter's bright,
In this wintry dance, oh what a sight!
So grab your mittens, join the parade,
For gliding on ice is a fun charade!

Frosty Follies

In my boots, I feel so grand,
Each step calculated, oh how planned!
But wait, what's this? A sneaky patch,
Out from under, my feet detach!

A little hop, a wobbly spin,
Trying to keep my balance in.
The world around me grins and bites,
As I twist and twirl in frosty tights.

With arms out wide, a superhero stance,
I'm destined to win this snowy dance.
Then a slip, a slide, it's such a sight,
As I tumble down with pure delight.

So chuckle with me, let's paint the scene,
On this ice, we reign like a queen!
With frosty follies, we write the tale,
Of winter's grip and our laughter's sail!

Steps of Serendipity

A glide of joy on icy trails,
With every waddle, humor prevails.
I'm the jester, the king of slips,
Acrobatics in winter's grips!

Each puff of air, an icy breath,
Dancing with danger, I tease with death.
But oh! What fun in this frozen play,
Who knew ice could melt fears away?

So here I go, with a hopeful twirl,
Spinning in circles, give it a whirl!
From stumble to stumble, laughter flows,
With every fall, my confidence grows.

Friends unite, the ice we charm,
Dodging falls, we mean no harm.
Steps of joy in this chilly spree,
Winter's playground, come dance with me!

Arctic Ballet of the Brave

In boots like tanks, we take our stance,
With flailing arms, we prance and dance.
The ice is slick, oh what a trip,
We wobble and spin, our confidence a blip.

Like penguins clad in daring flight,
We scamper left, then skid to right.
Each step we take, a conquest grand,
As laughter rings across the land.

A balancing act from circus shows,
With landmines of ice that nobody knows.
We tumble and laugh, it's part of the game,
In this frosty playground, we're all the same.

So grab a friend, join the ballet,
We'll glide and slide until the day.
With senses sharp and spirits high,
We're masters of ice, oh me, oh my!

Winter's Path of Wit

Careful steps, like tiptoeing mice,
Each crunch and crack, a roll of dice.
The ground feels wet but it's frozen tight,
We'll fashion boots that defy the night.

One step forward, then a graceful sway,
Oh look, dear friend, we're off the way!
With every slip, our pride is bruised,
But laughter's a balm that leaves us amused.

We gather as a goofy crew,
Cheering on each slip and skew.
With every slide, we let out a cheer,
As winter's stage holds us so dear.

So wear your best and let's collide,
On paths of ice, let's take this ride.
We'll dance till dawn, oh what a sight,
With snowflakes twirling, we take to flight!

Shimmery Steps Through Time

In frosty air, we make our mark,
Like slippery fish in a frozen park.
One step, two steps, oh what a thrill,
As gravity plays a game of skill.

We pirouette on panels of ice,
With moments bright and movements nice.
Sometimes we glide, sometimes we flop,
As laughter erupts with every drop.

It's a time machine, this winter floor,
Whirling us back to fun times before.
Each wobbly step, a tale anew,
With friendly falls that come in view.

So grab your pals and take a whirl,
In this season's funky, frozen twirl.
We'll dance through winter, smiles so wide,
On shimmery paths, let's take this ride!

Descending Into Frost

Oh how we plunge, with legs like jelly,
Into a world where the ice is smelly.
With careful grins and shifty feet,
We'll conquer the chill on this slippery street.

An icy slide, a frosty pit,
Where tumbleweeds and laughter fit.
With arms outstretched, we wrestle fate,
As gravity serves up a fancy plate.

Frames of joy in frosty displays,
As we slip and bounce through this wintry maze.
Each slide a giggle, each fall a sign,
That fun is found in the most dire lines.

So join the fun, don't hesitate,
A wobbly dance awaits, so great.
In this cold embrace, we find our way,
With merry hearts we'll laugh and play!

Icy Ballet of Balance

On crystal floors, we take our stance,
With wobbly legs, we dare to dance.
Arms flail wildly, a comical sight,
As we glide and slip in morning light.

A pirouette turns into a fall,
We laugh and giggle, all for the thrill.
Like penguins strutting, we shimmy and slide,
Who knew such chaos could bring such pride?

Snowflakes twirl in the chilly breeze,
While we grasp at air, attempting to please.
The ballet of winter is slippery fun,
As we tumble and roll, till the dance is done.

With each step taken, we laugh through the plight,
Making memories in this frosty delight.
So grab your friends, let's find a way,
To dance on this ice, come what may!

Crystalline Stumbles

A frosty path, inviting glints,
With shoes that squeak and pants that hint.
We sway like reeds in a winter's song,
Stumbling about, where we don’t belong.

Each step we take feels like a prank,
As if the ice has plans to tank.
One moment graceful, the next a fall,
Our giggles echo, the best of all.

With hats askew and cheeks aglow,
The slippery dance begins to flow.
Hold onto laughter, let fears dissipate,
For icy missteps will always create.

Round and round, we spin out of sync,
On this frozen pond, we all rethink.
A comical tableau, our breath clouds the air,
As we weave through stumbles, without a care!

Choreography of Cold Steps

In boots so bold, we strut and sway,
On this icy stage, we frolic and play.
Each step a challenge, each turn a test,
As we try to show off, only to jest.

With arms out wide, we mimic a bird,
Though landing softly feels absurd.
The ice it teases, with each little shift,
A clumsy ballet, like a cosmic gift.

A slip leads to laughter, a tumble to cheer,
As we dance on the ice with nothing to fear.
Like slapstick actors on a frozen set,
With each fail, another giggle is met.

Together we stumble, together we laugh,
In this frozen fiasco, we find our path.
So take off your cares, let the cold winds blow,
For the dance of the frosty is all about flow!

Winter's Slippery Serenade

The world is a wonder of white and blue,
As we step on the surface, a slippery hue.
Caught in a moment of icy delight,
We’re serenading winter, both day and night.

With each little step, we wobble and shake,
Like cartoons on ice, we’re hard to mistake.
Our boots are our partners, they twist and they turn,
While we plot our next move, there’s so much to learn.

A pratfall here with a giggle there,
The cold gives us thrills, but beware the glare!
For every laugh, there’s a chance to fall,
In this frosty ballet, we’ve answered the call.

So let’s raise a toast to the slips and the trips,
To the ice beneath and the laughter that rips.
For in this cold dance, we’ve truly excelled,
In the symphony of winter, we stumble and meld!

Frozen Flourish

Slip and slide, what a sight,
Legs a-flail in morning light.
Laughing hard with every fall,
Ice is sneaky, I recall.

Crunchy sound beneath my feet,
Made my morning feel complete.
Dancing like a silly clown,
Gonna show this ice who's clown!

Froze my toes, oh what a thrill,
Giggling, I must take a chill.
With each step, I lose my grace,
Oh dear, look at my red face!

Grab the rail, or else I'll fall,
Snowflakes join the slapstick ball.
Graceful? Nah, more like a mess,
Ice, you sly old frosty pess!

Winter's Rhythm

Two left feet, I can't go straight,
Whirling round like roller skate.
Watch me dance, I'll catch some air,
Oh no! Down, without a care!

Frosty winds blow with a laugh,
Sliding down this icy path.
With a twist and a silly hop,
Careful not to make a stop!

Cold and chilly on my nose,
Waddling like a penguin goes.
Steps so funny, I just grin,
Never thought I'd look like kin!

Frozen feels and laughter bright,
Let's embrace this frosty fight.
Fun and joy, oh what a blast,
Ice, you bring me good times fast!

Footprints in Frozen Echoes

Tiptoe lightly, oops, I slide,
Chasing laughter, oh what pride.
Footprints scattered, a wiggly trail,
Winter antics never fail!

Chilly breeze and giggles loud,
Who knew ice could draw a crowd?
Falling fast, yet loving each thud,
Whirls of snow, in winter's flood.

Pale blue sky, my arms out wide,
Fallen snow becomes my slide.
Echoes of laughter fill the air,
As my body meets with care.

Gliding through this winter spree,
Not quite graceful, but carefree.
Slip and slide, life’s funky dance,
Give the ice a funny chance!

The Art of Icy Walking

Step by step, with tiny prance,
Wobbling feet in frosty dance.
Laughing as I take a fall,
This big oaf's having a ball!

Cautiously I start to glide,
While the icy world, it does bide.
Arms go flailing, what a sight,
Winter’s laughter feels so right!

Silly as a playful pup,
With each slip, I just erupt.
Giggling hard as friends all cheer,
“Look at you, oh how sincere!”

Snowflakes whirl like tiny sprites,
Joyful shouts on frosty nights.
The ground beneath feels like a tease,
Yet I dance with goofy ease!

Nature’s Slippery Playground

On frozen paths, we brave the slick,
With every step, it feels like a trick.
We dance and slide, a comical sight,
In nature’s playground, we twirl with delight.

Snowflakes laugh as they tumble down,
While we slip and slide all over town.
It's a game of balance, give it a try,
Watch out for penguins, they might just fly!

With arms out wide, we begin the chase,
And hope that our feet can keep up the pace.
With every near-fall, our laughter grows loud,
In this slippery world, we feel so proud.

So grab your scarf and lace up those shoes,
Embrace the adventure, there's nothing to lose.
When life hands you ice, dance with abandon,
In nature's playground, join the grand stand-on!

Harmonizing with the Cold

In a frosty world, we learn a new jig,
With toes that feel like they’re stuck to a twig.
We waltz and we wobble, each step a delight,
Harmonizing with winter, oh what a sight!

The air is crisp, our cheeks rosy bright,
As we glide like swans, full of sheer fright.
We grin through the slips, stumble, and laugh,
Each frozen misstep is part of the path.

Snowmen chuckle, watching our spree,
Shovels and sleds, our friends, can't you see?
With a hop and a skip, we carry the glee,
Nature’s cool rhythms, a dance, wild and free.

So come take a chance on this slippery floor,
Grab a friend or two, and then just explore.
For in every slip, a memory we mold,
With laughter and joy, let the stories unfold!

Woven Together by Winter's Breath

Bundled up tight like a careless burrito,
We shuffle and slide, a clumsy little fleet though.
With layers of wool and hats asked to stay,
Every frosty moment becomes a ballet.

Fingers that freeze but spirits that soar,
We conquer ice patches, who could ask for more?
The sound of our laughter echoes so clear,
A tapestry woven with joy this time of year.

A slip here and there, our balance a mess,
But look at the joy, we couldn't care less.
With giggles and warmth in our hearts tightly sewn,
This icy adventure feels like our own.

So let’s make a pact as the chilly winds blow,
We’ll tackle this ice, as we twirl to and fro.
Together we’ll skate through this brisk winter’s breath,
Creating warm memories, defying the death!

A Journey Through the Crystal Maze

A glimmering path leads us here with a wink,
With sharp little natures, we tumble and sink.
Through a maze of crystals, we boldly roam,
Even if we slip, we still feel at home.

Hands in our pockets, we shuffle along,
Conversations echo like a joyful song.
With each icy twist and each turn that we take,
Our journey grows sweeter, with every heartache.

Like seals on a perch, we giggle and sway,
Together in chaos, we dance and we play.
With snowflakes as confetti, what a grand chase,
In this crystal maze, we find our own grace.

So slip and slide into the magic tonight,
In this wintry wonderland, everything's right.
With zany adventures bound tightly in smiles,
We'll conquer this maze and sail on for miles!

Navigating the Crystal Canvas

Upon the frozen ground we tread,
With cautious steps, a careful spread.
Our feet like penguins, waddle wide,
As laughter echoes far and wide.

Chin up high, we strut, we sway,
Flailing arms, come what may!
We shuffle, slide, oh what a sight,
Attempting grace on ice so bright.

Each stumble met with giggles loud,
As icy crowns we all avowed.
A slip, a fall, then back we rise,
With gleeful shouts that touch the skies.

Living art on this slick stage,
Our chilly dance, we perform with gage.
Oh, how we glide, oh, how we slip,
In this frozen world, we take our trip.

Dance of the Icebound Feet

With boots a-flop and heart afire,
We take to ice, our feet conspire.
A pirouette here, a twirl gone wrong,
In this icy land, we all belong.

We spin and slide, a clumsy crew,
With winter's grip, we bid adieu.
Arms like windmills, legs like clay,
In this frosty ballet, we play.

Giggles erupt with every fall,
We gather up, we stand up tall.
A tangled heap, we laugh and scream,
As ice beneath becomes our dream.

Around we whirl with joyful shouts,
Like human skids, we bounce about.
In every twist and every bend,
Our frosty frolics never end.

Frosty Footfalls

Step by step, we venture forth,
The ground below, a shiny north.
Watch your toes, dear friend of mine,
For this slippery surface is quite divine.

A little hop and then a glide,
Our careful ways we cannot hide.
But with each slip, a burst of glee,
We dance like stars on a frozen spree.

Chattering teeth and icy noses,
We dodge the falls like fearless roses.
Our laughter cuts through winter's chill,
As we prance wildly, against our will.

With frosty footfalls, we skip along,
Making memories where we belong.
One brave leap, then down we go,
In this silly dance on ice and snow.

Whispering Icicles

With each cautious step, a story told,
Of frosty slips and laughter bold.
As icicles whisper their chilly song,
We waddle forth, and we can't go wrong.

Tiny tottles, here and there,
A skateboard ride through icy air.
With arms akimbo, we brave the slide,
In this winter waltz, we take our pride.

We laugh at tumbles, the moments spare,
As frozen water fills the air.
Like clumsy ducks, we quack with glee,
In this icefield, wild and free.

In shimmering chaos, we find our groove,
As chilly challenges make us move.
Hold on tight, it’s quite the show,
In this frosty whirlwind, let’s go!

Balancing Act Beneath the Sky

Tiptoe on the frozen glint,
Like a penguin set to sprint.
Elbows out, don’t look down,
Laughing, sliding all around.

Skates or boots, what’s your flair?
Whirling 'round without a care.
Foot to foot, a comical stride,
Grinning wide, it’s quite the ride!

Catch a friend with arms so wide,
Who knew ice could be this slick?
Tumbles feel like jest, you see,
Just giggles on the frosted sea.

Waddles loud, it’s quite a sight,
Racing moonbeams, deep in night.
If you slip, just take a bow,
Be the star of ice, somehow!

Frosted Pathways

On frosty ground, we dance and swerve,
Hilarity from each little curve.
Did I just twirl? Oh what a show!
Here comes the wind, let's sway and flow!

Frozen dreams beneath my feet,
Skipping whims, a frosty beat.
Giggles spring from every fall,
Balancing acts enthrall us all.

Every glide, a slip of grace,
I’ll join the circus, take my place!
If life gets slippery, make it fun,
With squeals and laughter, we have won!

Join the chaos, let it be,
Waddle on, just wait and see.
In this ballet of ice and cheer,
We find our fun, year after year!

Moonlit Glides

Under moonlight, we boldly stray,
Sliding sideways, hey, what a way!
With every step, a giggle reigns,
As frosty air whisks away our pains.

How do you balance? It's pure delight,
A sudden slip? Just take flight!
Cracking up on this chilly floor,
Who knew ice could bring such lore?

Shimmies, shakes, a twirl or two,
With rubbery legs, we break right through.
In a world where spills mean smiles,
We skate through winter's chilly trials.

With friends near, we laugh and play,
Fools of frost, come what may.
For every fall, a story shared,
On icy paths, love is declared!

Echoes of Winter Wisdom

They say the secrets lie in the glide,
But I'm more of a tumble and slide.
Each waddle's a tale from the frost,
Of laughter found, never lost.

With wisdom from a frostbitten sage,
I shuffle like a cartoon page.
Feet like rubber, heart full of glee,
Join the circus, come walk with me!

Twists and turns, oh what a thrill,
Balance is no big deal – just sit still!
But if you dare to dance tonight,
Wear a helmet; it's quite the flight!

Winter's charm is a comedy,
Where every misstep's done with glee.
So slip away, let laughter reign,
On these icy paths, we'll dance again!

Tread Gently on Glassy Surfaces

With care I take my shuffling stride,
Each step a dance with fate, oh my!
The ground beneath a frosty glide,
I teeter, swirl, then slowly fly!

Arms out wide like flailing wings,
A penguin's grace, I try to claim,
But down I go—oh what fun things!
A slip of pride and face in shame!

My boots like ice skates, they do spin,
A shimmy here, and then a glide,
The world looks on, where to begin?
A comedy show on nature's slide!

I laugh aloud, my ego bruised,
As snowflakes fall in joyful cheer,
For falling down, I'm thus infused,
With giggles that the brave hold dear!

Dancing with the Icy Breeze

In chilly air, my boots take flight,
I leap and bounce, so full of glee,
A cha-cha here, a twirl just right,
Dear ice, please don't swallow me!

Each step a page from slapstick tales,
With wobbling knees, I dance askew,
Like baby deer, my balance fails,
Yet laughter echoes—yes, that's true!

I spin like a ballerina bold,
While gravity plays an ugly game,
Cackles around me, uncontrolled,
Oh joy, this cold has brought me fame!

Embracing falls, my heart now flies,
For every slip, there's joy entwined,
And as I dance, the world complies,
In icy bliss, I lose my mind!

Steps in a Shimmering Wonderland

In this frosty realm, I trot with flair,
Each step a stomp, a leap, a spin,
With every crack, I stop and stare,
As glistening shards call me to win!

My boots encased in glitter trails,
Sprinkled sparkles, a sight to see,
But oh, beware those sneaky hails,
For ice can turn to sly decree!

Wobble left and glide to the right,
I'm a jester on slippery ground,
Fingers crossed, I wish to take flight,
While people giggle at my sound!

The world is bright, though balance low,
Each slip a chance to play and fall,
With joy I revel in the show,
A merry dancer—step, hop, enthrall!

Navigating the Frostbitten Labyrinth

In a maze of ice, my feet won’t listen,
Like noodles flopping, I have no clue,
Through twists and turns, my hopes are glisten,
Each wobble tells me this won't do!

Skates or no, I bob and weave,
A circus act on frozen tracks,
With every shudder, I just believe,
That humor hides in all my cracks!

Oh look, a snowman! Time to slide,
With grace of an elephant, I zoom,
Each movement's like a wild joyride,
And laughter follows 'round the room!

At last I'm free—wait, where's the door?
The ice has claimed my sense of space!
Through giggles loud, I shout for more,
As winter's maze becomes my grace!

Sliding on Crystal Paths

I step outside, it’s pure delight,
A glimmering stage, oh what a sight!
With my arms out wide, I brave the cold,
Pretending I’m graceful, or so I’m told.

But one little slip, I start to spin,
It feels like a dance, but where do I begin?
With a hop and a skip, I slide like a pro,
Or maybe I’m just putting on a show!

I watch my friends, they don’t seem aware,
Of the icy traps that lurk everywhere.
They run with great speed, with confidence high,
While I just chuckle and give it a try.

So here’s to the joy of that frozen fling,
As we skate through the winter, let laughter ring!
Embrace all the tumbles and giggles galore,
Each slip is a story, who could ask for more?

Grace in Frosty Footfalls

In heavy boots, I make my way,
Each step like a game, will I sway?
With my feet splayed wide like a bird in flight,
The ground laughs beneath, oh what a sight!

A tiptoe here, a shuffle there,
I catch a glance, I start to stare.
The art of slipping, I try to finesse,
But I end up tangled in my own mess!

The ice is a joker, a slippery friend,
It sends me flying around the bend.
But with each pratfall, I find my cheer,
This chilly ballet brings folks near.

So dance like a penguin, embrace the thrill,
Laugh 'til you cry, let slip and spill!
Frosty footfalls may make us fall,
But the joy of the season beats one and all!

Gliding Through the Frozen Silence

The world is a canvas, white and bright,
I waddle outside in the sparkle of light.
Beneath me, the ice, oh so sly,
Each step a puzzle, oh me, oh my!

With a laugh in my throat, I take a step slow,
Will I glide effortlessly, or eat icy snow?
Feet glued like clowns to a slippery stage,
Each graceful attempt turns into a rage!

A freeze and a flail, I attempt to execute,
But balance, dear friend, is quite astute.
So I wobble and wave, like a fish out of stream,
In a glorious dance, I slip – then I beam!

The frozen silence bursts with glee,
I'm not the best skater, but I'm wild and free.
With giggles and grins, I embrace each fall,
Winter's a rollercoaster, come one, come all!

Echoes of a Slippery Stroll

With courage in heart and a wit that's sly,
I take on the ice on a frosty high.
Each step a whisper, a laugh in the air,
As I navigate paths with utmost care.

The wind sings a tune, a slippery song,
While I choose my spots, oh so wrong!
A little too far, and there I go,
Into an unplanned slide, oh what a show!

The echoes of laughter resonate wide,
As I tumble and roll, there's no place to hide.
A dance on the ice, so wild and free,
With each little slip, I'm just me!

So gather 'round friends, come share in the fun,
With each frosty stroll, there's joy to be won.
For in the great slip, there's freedom to find,
Just let yourself go, leave worries behind!

Navigating the Glacial Garden

Step by step on icy ground,
Watch your feet; they might rebound.
A slip here, a slide there,
You're dancing like you just don't care.

Penguins giggle; they've got style,
While you flail and twist a while.
Grab a railing, hold it tight,
Who knew ice could be such a fright?

With a wobble, a hop, and a glide,
You'll turn an ice pond into a ride.
So here we go, one more chance,
Let's risk it all in this frozen dance.

Frosty air and giggles ring,
Life's a circus—let's all swing!
So don that scarf and raise your voice,
On this slick stage, we rejoice!

Ballet on the Shimmering Ice

Twirl and spin in frozen grace,
Oh dear, there goes my face!
A pirouette and a sudden drop,
Hoping I don’t faceplant; oh, stop!

The ice it glitters, oh so bright,
But underfoot, it’s quite a fright.
I glide and wobble, what a scene!
Am I a dancer or just obscene?

With balletic poise, I give a flutter,
But down I go, it’s like soft butter.
A giggle echoing from afar,
Is that my friend or a tiny star?

Such elegance and style I crave,
But all I find’s a frosty grave.
So leap and laugh, it's quite a play,
Ballet on ice is here to stay!

Slipping on Frozen Dreams

In my shoes, ice greets my feet,
A frosty mess; I can't compete.
With a hop and a jump, I try my best,
But oh, the tumbling has no rest!

Each step I take's a wild debut,
I'm a star in a comedy to view.
A slip, a slide, a startled shout,
This frozen ground's what life's about!

Ice-kissed wishes, oh so slick,
I try to stand, but it's quite a trick.
Like a show on the late-night screen,
I slip and slide, it's all routine.

Laughing hard with every fall,
It's not graceful, but oh, how I enthrall!
So gather round, and let's embrace,
These frozen dreams in a thrilling race!

Glide of Graceful Frost

The morning chill bites my toes,
With each brave step, excitement grows.
Treading lightly on this sheet,
I wave to friends as I dance on fleet.

A flash of humor in every trip,
As I take a wobbly dip.
They're cheering me from the sides,
As I glide along on frosty rides.

The ice beneath is slick and sly,
I land like a bird, oh so shy.
But laughter bubbles with every tumble,
What a joyful, icy jumble!

So come and join this frozen spree,
Where slip-ups turn to jubilee.
With giggles shared and frosty cheer,
Let's make sweet memories here, my dear!

Frigid Footwork

Slippers so sleek, I take a bold chance,
One wrong move and I'm lost in a dance.
Legs spread wide like a stork in a spin,
Oh, how I wish I had practiced within!

My feet are like fish, slipping and sliding,
With every step, my courage colliding.
I waddle and shuffle, a sight to behold,
Laughter erupts as my pride turns to gold.

Falling is part of this icy ballet,
The ground has its charm in its own funny way.
Chasing my balance on an ice-colored stage,
I tumble with grace, like a performer uncaged.

With each little wobble, a giggle ignites,
Fashion icons in hats that look trite.
I'll master the slide, come celebrate me,
The frosty fresh artist of slapstick glee!

The Poet's Glide

At dawn, I step onto the glass-like street,
My feet take a flight, oh, what a treat!
I scribble in rhythm, my pen takes a chance,
A slip of the toe sends me into a dance.

I glide like a poet on a slippery verse,
Struggling for balance, my steps are a curse.
With hip-hop flair and a classic approach,
I waddle and swirl like a quirky roach.

Imagine the audience, cheers on a drift,
The clumsy performance, I've surely a gift.
Footprints of laughter trail behind my show,
A frosty performance, come watch it glow!

Now watch my feet twirl, they tango, they spin,
The ice is my stage, let the frolic begin!
So raise up your mittens, let the applause fly,
For the poet who glides with a wink and a sigh!

Twirl of the Frosty Breeze

Amidst frosted mornings, boots armed for war,
I venture outside, but what lies in store?
The ground below gleams like a disco ball,
With a twirl and a slip, I teeter and fall.

Shoulders like penguins, they sway to the beat,
As I shuffle and shimmy, avoiding defeat.
The frost whispers secrets, I tumble and freeze,
Chasing my rhythm, like wind in the trees.

Giggles erupt from the crowd gathering 'round,
A ballet of balance, much laughter is found.
With frosty finesse and a twinkle of glee,
I rise up again, oh-so-fearless and free!

So hear the sweet music that ice underfoot plays,
As I twirl with abandon on those slippery rays.
t's dance through this winter, my friends, join the spree,

In the twirl of the breezy, frosty jubilee!

Icebound Melodies

Out on the pavement, so slick and so bright,
I venture with courage, my heart full of fright.
Each step is a gamble, a note in a song,
Hoping I won't do the ice dance too long.

With arms wide like airplanes, I take to the field,
My balance, quite wobbly, but laughter's my shield.
A step and a slide, my feet play a tune,
While neighbors peek out, looking up at the moon.

Oh jingle the laughter, the mischief around,
We waltz on the frosty, no serenade bound.
In this slippery realm, we men, women, glide,
Creating a harmony of frolic and ride.

So dance with abandon, let winters come play,
For every nice tumble turns troubles away.
With ice bound so tight, our joy is set free,
Melodies of laughter, come dance with me!

Navigating the Icy Veils

Step by step, oh so slow,
Wobbling feet, here we go!
Watch your step, don't lose the fight,
It's a dance, but not quite right.

One wrong move, a slip, a slide,
Grabbing friends on either side.
Elbows flailing, giggles erupt,
In icy paths, we're all corrupt!

Penguin shuffle, a sight to see,
Flapping arms like birds in glee.
Each cautious step, a game we play,
A chilly challenge, come what may!

With every glide, we trip and laugh,
Catching ice like a photograph.
So let's embrace this icy spree,
A frosty ballet, just wait and see!

Winter's Dance of Delight

Beneath a sky of icy blue,
We twirl and spin, as penguins do.
Slipping here, a nimble feet,
Falling down is quite the feat!

Snowflakes flutter all around,
As we progress, balance is found.
A waddle here, a sway, a glide,
Laughter echoes far and wide.

Grab your snacks, don’t let them fall,
Keep them safe while dodging it all.
A juggling act as we perform,
In this winter mix, we all transform!

So join the fun, release your fright,
Get ready for a slippery night.
With every laugh, we take a chance,
On the ice, we’ll find our dance!

Glide into Winter's Arms

With a whoosh and a screech, we navigate,
Trying to balance while feeling great.
Watch the ground, don't lose sight,
Or you'll be in for quite a fright!

Toe to heel, it's a funny sight,
Swaying like a wisp in flight.
Props to those who make it through,
With laughter shared by quite a crew!

Each tiny shift feels like a dream,
On this slippery, frosty theme.
Watch your step, here comes a slide,
Laughter echoes in our ride!

As we slip and stumble, all in sync,
We find the fun in each ice rink.
So join the dance, embrace the fall,
In the joyful grip of winter's call!

Shimmering Balance

Ice beneath, a glittering sheen,
We tiptoe gingerly, oh what a scene!
With squeals of glee and scattered woes,
We dance along where the frosty wind blows.

Who needs skates when you've got style?
With every trip, we flash a smile.
A wobbly grace we all possess,
In winter's grip, we feel no stress!

So throw on your coat, and grab your friends,
Every slip is a giggle, the fun never ends.
Look out below! We've lost our poise,
But in this chaos, we rejoice!

Just one more glide, one last spin,
Together we laugh—let's do it again!
With hearts so light and spirits high,
We conquer ice, don't ask us why!

Sashay on the Slick

With shoes like slicks, I take a chance,
My feet start sliding, it's quite the dance!
One foot adelante, then a quick retreat,
I’m an ice-skating penguin, quick on my feet.

With arms out wide, it's pure delight,
I'm a graceful swan, well, maybe not quite.
A little shimmy, then a mighty flail,
I hope to land, but oh, I must bail!

The ground below, a mirror's embrace,
Each step I take, it’s a hilarious race.
Giggles surround me, my steps like a joke,
Witness my splendor, I’m a slippery bloke.

A careful tiptoe, pretending I'm smooth,
But every loud crack makes me lose my groove.
In this frosty show, I’m the star of the show,
Just watch your step, or join in the flow!

Frigid Footprints

Tiptoe across this icy land,
Leaving behind a wobbly strand.
With each frozen step, laughter ignites,
Like a deer on skates, I fear for my rights.

A slip and a slide, oh what a thrill,
I'm channeling my inner seal, what a skill!
Carefully plotting each foot to the next,
This frosty adventure feels somewhat perplexed.

Watch those footprints, they weave and they dart,
My ice ballet is a work of art.
As I shimmy and shake, I fight to stay stout,
But gravity's laughing, it's taking me out!

A flurry of laughter now fills the cold air,
As I recover my stance with an awkward flair.
Each frigid footprint tells tales of my plight,
In this icy realm, oh what a funny sight!

Chilled Cadence

I step with caution, like a timid cat,
One foot at a time, like I’m wearing a hat.
The ground beneath me, it beckons to slip,
I’m ready for wobbles, but not for a trip!

Waddle like a duck, with style so keen,
I’m an ice explorer, a chill-seeking machine.
With steps that are bouncy and a heart that’s light,
I’m mastering moves in the frost's wicked bite.

Each slide is a giggle, each trip is a dance,
In this icy adventure, I take a chance.
A swirl and a twirl, oh look at me go,
I'm the comical king in this snowy casino!

With laughter contagious, I glide to the end,
My frigid cadence has become quite the trend.
In this slippery realm, joy takes the lead,
With ice as my stage, oh, what fun indeed!

Glimpse of Grace on Ice

In the frosty air, where laughter aligns,
I dance on the ice, with no sense of signs.
A graceful twirl? Oh no, just a flail,
But this comical tumble, it'll surely prevail!

What seems like poise, is a trick of the light,
As I stumble and bounce, oh what a sight!
With arms wide open, I'm a human kite,
A snapshot of grace that's just not quite right.

With every misstep, I just can't desist,
An icy ballet, with a flick of the wrist.
Laughter erupts, and I join in the fun,
In this slippery dance, I'm everyone's son!

So come take a glance at this chilly charade,
Where slips turn to smiles, and fears start to fade.
In the glimpse of grace on this frosty delight,
We all find our rhythm, in the moonlight so bright!

Arctic Elegance in Motion

I step like a penguin, so graceful and sly,
With flailing arms, and a hopeful sigh.
Each stride is a shuffle, a dance on the floor,
A slip and a slide, what's behind me? No more!

The ice glimmers bright, a stage set just right,
For clumsy performers to take on the night.
With a squeak and a slip, I'm an acrobat bold,
As I ply my frozen feet, oh behold!

The glances from snowmen as I take my grand bow,
Who knew this would happen?" they ask me somehow.
I'm the star of this show, in my bibbed and my boots,
With every misstep, I'm shaking my roots!

So here's to the laughter, the slips, and the falls,
To dancing on ice and hearing the calls.
For every small stumble provides the best cheer,
In Arctic elegance, have no fear, my dear!

Laughter in the Frigid Air

In the depths of the cold, with ice all around,
My feet turn to butter; I waddle, confound!
I flap like a seal, I fumble like mad,
Each step is a riddle, it drives me quite glad.

The snowflakes are chuckling, they dance all about,
While I do the tango, of that there's no doubt.
With a hop and a skip, on this glassy terrain,
I glide like a fish, in a humorous vein!

The dogs come to watch, they snicker with glee,
As I pirouette once—"Are we learning?" said he.
The joy of this chaos, oh, how can I miss?
As I tumble and roll, it feels just like bliss!

So come join the frolic, the laughter, the play,
Let's wobble together, in our merry ballet.
For when life's on thin ice, we giggle and cheer,
In the frigid air, there's nothing to fear!

Ballet of the Snowbound

A pirouette stumble, a two-step jive,
On this frozen stage, I feel so alive!
With grace like a cow, and style so divine,
I dance for my audience, a performance of mine.

Snowflakes applaud as I sashay and spin,
An ice ballet where few dare to begin.
With arms wide like wings, I'm a bird on a breeze,
Sharing my passion for laughter with ease.

The wind gives a whistle, it joins in the fun,
While neighbors peek out, "Oh look at her run!"
With every slip onward, my laughter erupts,
In my snow-shoe ballet, who cares if I'm cupped?

So here's to the wobbles, the giggles aplenty,
To dances in snow, quite shockingly hefty.
For in every misstep, there's joy to embrace,
In this ballet of ice, I'm in the right place!

Serenity on Shattered Glass

Oh, how I glide on this glistening sheet,
Like a graceful gazelle, oh must I concede!
One little slip sends me right on the back,
I'm serenely reminded, I need to keep track!

Each twirl is a laugh, a joke in disguise,
With moments of grace countered by surprise.
I slide like a seal, with a giggle and glide,
While the world keeps on spinning, I take it in stride

The trees hold their breath as I commence my dance
With arms flailing wildly, I seize my chance.
A flower of laughter blooms from the ground,
As I whirl and twirl, joy's ultimately found!

So cheer for the shivers, the slips in the cold,
For each frozen moment is a story retold.
Serenity's laughter is the warmth that we seek,
As we waddle through winter, let's share and not pee

K
roup UK Ltd.
124
12B/563

9 789916 9419